ALL ABOUT

My Pet Dog

Our Life Together

My Name: _______________________

My Age: _______________________

My Dog's Name and Age:

____

My Dog's Breed:

____

Veterinarian's Name: 

____

When I first saw you ...

Your Home:

Your favorite comforts:

I chose your name because ...

____

____

____

____

I think your name suits you because ...

____

____

____

____

Drawing

When I am with you I feel ...

Our first photo together is:

If I could ask you one
question it would be ...

____

____

____

____

I would like to know
this because ...

____

____

____

____

Your favorite food is:

Your diet is:

The funny things you do ...

Our life together ...

I can tell when you are happy because ...

____

____

____

____

____

____

____

____

I can tell when you are scared because …

____

____

____

____

____

____

Together we can ...

The places we go ...

Something I have learned from you is ...

____

____

____

____

____

____

____

On your Birthday ...

Your favorite thing to do is …

You have learned how to ...

I love you because ...

____

____

____

____

____

____

____

____

____

A happy memory:

My favorite photo of us is:

Favorite Keepsake